JONATHAN AND ANGELA SCOTT

TIGERS
OF RANTHAMBORE

CAMBRIDGE
UNIVERSITY PRESS

UCL
Institute of Education

Jonathan and Angie Scott are photographers. They travel around the world taking pictures of animals. One of their favourite places is Ranthambore [*Ran – tham – bor*] National Park in North India. It is one of the best places in the world to see tigers in the wild. There are many other animals in the park, too.

Jonathan and Angie Scott

Ranthambore National Park in the early morning

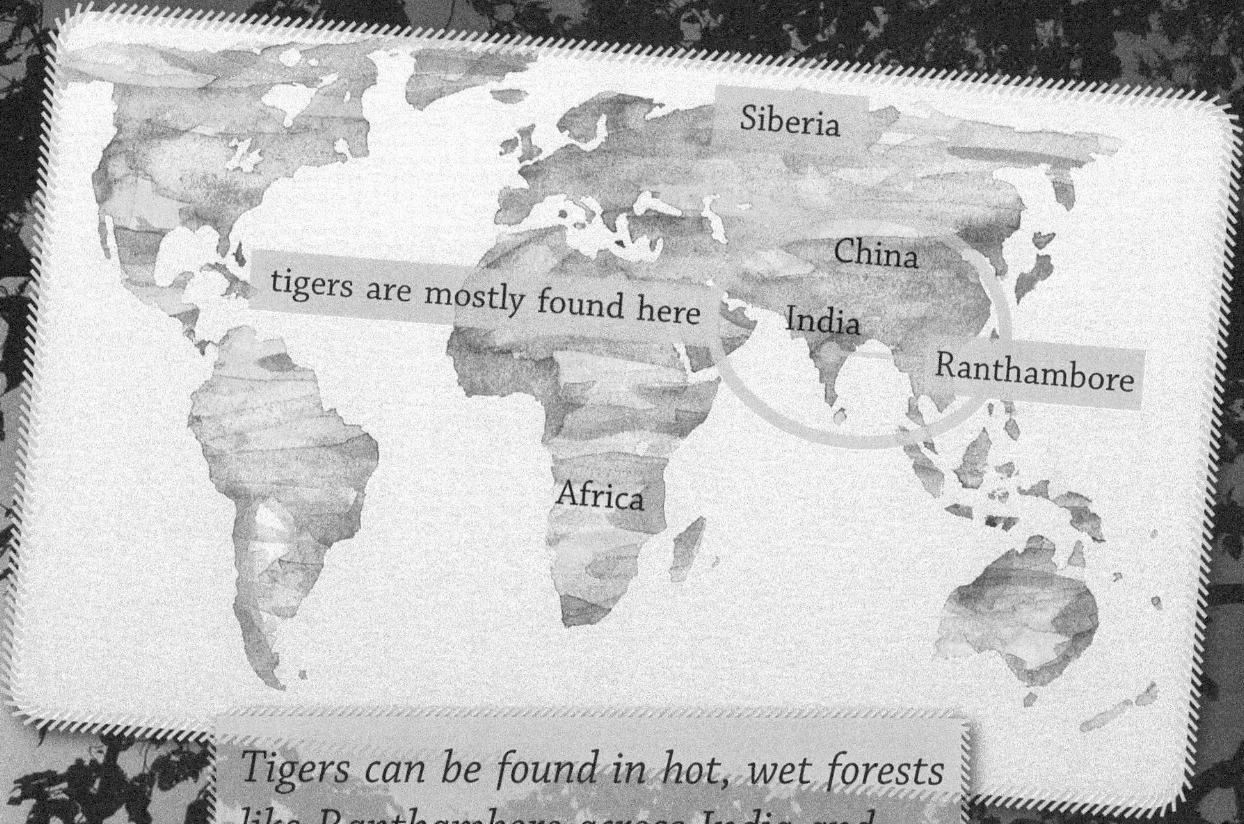

Siberia

China

India

tigers are mostly found here

Ranthambore

Africa

Tigers can be found in hot, wet forests like Ranthambore across India and Asia. But they live in many different habitats. Siberian Tigers live in the snowy mountains of Siberia.

3

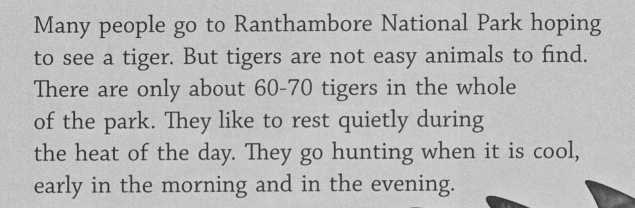

Many people go to Ranthambore National Park hoping to see a tiger. But tigers are not easy animals to find. There are only about 60-70 tigers in the whole of the park. They like to rest quietly during the heat of the day. They go hunting when it is cool, early in the morning and in the evening.

Visitors to the park must travel about with a guide in a special car.

When people go in through the gates of the park, the first animals they will see are langurs, begging for food from the crowd. Langurs are a kind of monkey. They have learned how to get food in lots of clever ways.

Langurs spend some of the time on the ground and some in the trees.

Tigers are the biggest of all the cats, bigger even than lions. The Siberian tiger can grow up to 3 metres long and weigh 300 kilograms.

Tigers mark their **territory** by scratching trees and leaving their scent on the trunks. This way, they leave 'messages' for each other. They also roar to 'talk' to each other over long distances. But tigers cannot purr to show they are happy. When they are relaxed, they just shut their eyes.

Tigers prefer going out in the evening, rather than in the middle of the night. Their eyesight is very good. It is about six times better than a human's.

During the heat of the day, the tigers are resting. It is too hot to hunt. They wait in the shadows until it is cooler. The visitors are more likely to see the other animals in the park.

SEEING ANIMALS IN THE PARK

Spotted deer live all around the park. They are very shy. The spots on their coats help them to move between the trees without being seen.

There is another kind of deer. Sambar are much bigger than the Spotted deer. They are also bolder.

8

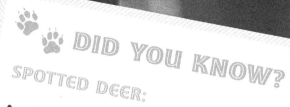

DID YOU KNOW?

SPOTTED DEER:

- are smaller and lighter.
- live in **herds**.
- are hunted by many **predators**, like tigers and crocodiles.

SAMBAR:

- are bigger and heavier.
- live in herds, but males can also live by themselves.
- are hunted by tigers.

This family of Sambar have come to the river to drink.

Other creatures watch out for predators.
The peacock quickly shuts his tail and makes a noise
to warn other birds. It sounds like a trumpet.
He knows that there is a tiger close by.

PEACOCKS:

- have long tails, called 'trains'.
- open their tails and **display** them to attract females. Females are called peahens.
- can fly, although not very far.
- sleep in small trees at night.

A dhole is a wild dog. They sometimes follow tigers, hoping to pick up scraps after the tigers have finished eating. The dholes have to be careful not to be seen.

Wild boars also need to be careful. A tiger could be hiding in the grass.

Wild boars have sharp **tusks**. *They can be fierce, but a tiger can catch a boar and eat it.*

11

SEEING A TIGER

If the visitors are lucky, they may catch sight of a tiger. This young male tiger is watching his prey but it looks as if he is relaxing amongst the trees.

His stripy coat blends in perfectly with the sunlight and shadows. This **camouflage** helps him creep up on prey, like young deer and wild boar.

THE QUEEN OF TIGERS

The oldest tiger in the park is called Machali. She has lived in Ranthambore for 20 years. The normal **lifespan** for a tiger in the wild is about 12–15 years.

Many of the tigers in the park are her children and grandchildren.

Machali is famous for her courage. She was once spotted winning a fight with a crocodile. She is also famous for **protecting** her cubs from danger.

People call her the Queen of the Park because she has been so important to the Tigers of Ranthambore.

In order to know if the tigers are nearby, the rangers in the park look for huge tiger footprints, called pugmarks. This one is bigger than a man's hand.

15

As the afternoon gets cooler, a tigress and her daughter come down to the lake to drink. Later, they might go in the water. Tigers can swim. It helps them cool down and sometimes they catch fish to eat.

🐾 🐾 DID YOU KNOW?

A TIGRESS:

- is a female tiger.
- usually has a **litter** of 2-4 cubs.
- has her cubs with her until they are around 18 months or 2 years old

16

Crocodiles wait in the water until they see something small enough to catch easily. They often hunt for fish. But crocodiles will not attack tigers. They are too big and powerful.

As evening comes, the tigers wait by the waterhole beneath Ranthambore's ancient fort. They keep a lookout for other animals who come down to the water to drink.

The park gets its name from the fort as sits on top of the Thambhore hill, looking down on the river Rann.

Hunters try and catch tigers because they can get a lot of money for a tiger skin. They will sell the skins to make rugs and clothes.

Many forests and jungles have been used to build houses, farms and factories. Tigers die because they have nowhere to live. They also get killed by farmers protecting their farm because tigers sometimes attack livestock.

Tigers are an **endangered** species. This means that there will soon be no more tigers in the wild unless people stop killing them. There are only about 3,500 left.

Ranthambore National Park at sunset

The sun is setting. A tiger roars in the distance. Squawks and howls from other animals can be heard. The tigers will soon be setting out to hunt.

It is time for visitors to leave the park.

GLOSSARY

camouflage: colours and patterns which make it hard to see the animal

dappled: marked with light coloured spots

display: show off

endangered: in danger of becoming extinct

herds: groups of animals living together

industry: making things for money

lifespan: length of life

litter: group of animal babies

packs: groups of dogs

predators: animals that hunt

prey: animals that are hunted

protecting: looking after

territory: area of land that an animal feels it owns

tusks: long teeth which stick out

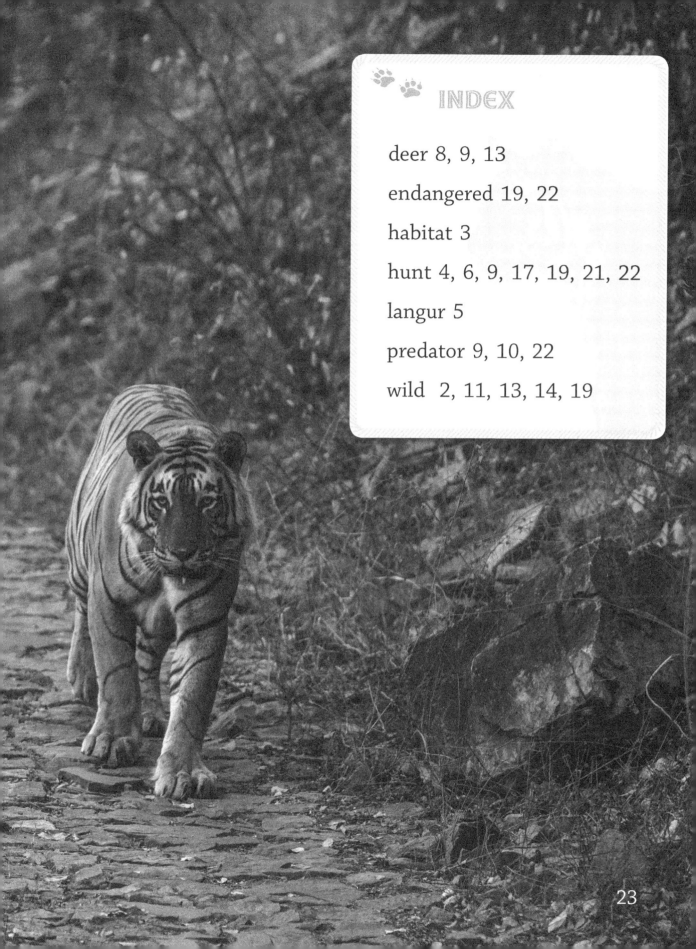

TIGERS OF RANTHAMBORE — JONATHAN & ANGELA SCOTT

Teaching notes written by Sue Bodman and Glen Franklin

Using this book

Developing reading comprehension

This non-fiction report focuses on the tigers of Ranthambore National Park in India. The reader is taken through a day in the park and the animals that a typical visitor might see. A glossary supports comprehension of technical and specific vocabulary.

Grammar and sentence structure

- Sentences follow the grammatical conventions of reports by using the present tense.
- Bullet points are used in the facts boxes.
- Complex sentences with two or more clauses support the development of comprehension.

Word meaning and spelling

- Place names and animal names introduce less familiar spelling patterns.
- The glossary and fact boxes are used to develop vocabulary.

Curriculum links

Conservation – National parks are set up to preserve wildlife and cultural heritage. Children can select a national park close to their locality and investigate why it was set up and what species and ecosystem it was set up to preserve.

Literacy – The book reports on how tigers spend their time, through the day and into the night. Children could create a tiger schedule to present what tigers are doing throughout a 24 hour period.

Learning Outcomes

Children can:

- skim-read illustrations and sub-headings to speculate what the book might be about
- adapt to different text types with growing flexibility
- solve most unfamiliar words on-the-run by blending less common digraphs
- pose questions prior to reading non-fiction and record these in writing, to find answers
- locate parts of the text that give particular information.

A guided reading lesson

Book Introduction

Give a copy of the book to each child. Have them read the title and the blurb independently.

Orientation

Ask: *What type of text do you think this is?* Clarify that it is an information text and ask the children to point out the key features that indicate this is non-fiction. Ask the children to give some information that they know about tigers. Use their responses to model asking questions about the topic. For example, *Sam said he thinks that tigers eat grass as well as meat. I'm not sure about that. I'd like to find out whether this is true.* Give out paper or note books and ask the children to jot down some questions about tigers that they would like to find out.

Preparation

Read the title. Ask: *Why do you think the book is called 'The Tigers of Ranthambore'?* In order to establish that the tigers in the book are located in specific place.

Have the children read pages 2 and 3 independently. Then discuss the setting and the role of the authors. Show how additional information in given in the label to the map on page 3. Look at how unfamiliar words have a pronunciation guide and they will help say the word correctly. Practice using the syllable chunks to read the unfamiliar name of the park.

Page 4 – Ask the children to read page 4 to themselves in order to find out when the visitors are most likely to see the tigers.

Pages 8 and 9 – Tell the children that visitors to the park will see other animals as well. Demonstrate the use of the fact box, and how the information in bullet points is read like a list.

Set a purpose for reading: *You are going to read this book to find out the answers to your questions. As you read, think about how you will need to use the contents, glossary and index to help you. Don't forget to look in the fact boxes, too.*